# The Moguls, Miners
# And Mistresses
# of Cleopatra Hill

Sedona, AZ

D1193478

I

*(Dedication)*

To the Miners, Lawmen, Pioneers,
Pony Soldiers and People of the Sun
of the Verde Valley

*Editor:* Aliza Caillou
*Historic Maps:* Reed Thorne
*Cover and Interior Design:* Ron Henry Design
*Printed by:* Media Lithographics
Sacramento, CA, C. Penny Callmeyer

ISBN 978-0-935810-77-6  paperback

Copyright 1990 Thorne Enterprises Publications
2nd Printing 1995
3rd Printing 2003

# "HIZZONER" The Governor, "BAKING POWDER" Bill And "RAWHIDE" Jimmy: The Men Who Built Jerome

## Jerome's Mining History To The Great Depression

### By Jeanette Rodda

early two hundred years before American colonists declared their independence from England, Europeans rode into Central Arizona's lush Verde Valley in search of silver and gold. These imperious Spanish conquistadores, dispatched from Mexico City, commanded trains of common soldiers, native guides and bearers, priests, and assorted camp followers, penetrating north as far as modern Kansas. The conquistadore, Antonio de Espejo, first European to explore the Verde Valley, found native Yavapai Indians engaged in exploiting the region's mineral wealth in 1583. Yavapai men, women, and children, wearing crosses tied in their hair, led Espejo along a steep mountain trail high above the valley floor to a mineralized outcrop of rock. Here he observed native miners working above ground and in tunnels, chiseling off richly-colored blue and green pigments with stone tools; dyes from the pigments decorated bodies, clothing, blankets, and utensils. Over four-hundred years later, the outcrop marked the site of the richest individually-owned copper mine in the world.

Espejo later toured underground salt mines on the valley floor, from which the Yavapais extracted this valuable mineral for local use and trade. Early twentieth-century miners working these mines sometimes discovered grisly reminders of their ancient counterparts: skeletons preserved in salt; the fossilized bones of a human hand and forearm at a depth of seventy feet; and a skull split in two by a stone hammer.

The Spaniards left the valley to the Yavapai and did not return. Abundant water, arable soil, and potential native converts and workers did not interest them with no gold or silver in the bargain. Espejo sought neither prime settlement land nor copper. He complained in his journal of the high copper content of the outcrop, how it obscured and locked in meager streaks of silver and gold. Only modern smelting methods would release the wealth of precious metals embedded in the rich copper ore: eighteen and a half million ounces of silver and over half a million ounces of gold by 1922.

The Yavapai saw no more whites in their valley until the early nineteenth century when white trappers, including Kit Carson and the tragic-comic James Ohio Pattie, moved in and cleared the Verde River of beaver. Like the conquistadores, these colorful and destructive individuals moved on quickly. The close of the Civil War brought a third wave of whites. Mainly Anglo-American farmers and ranchers, they pushed into the valley from the Territorial capital at Prescott, eager to graze their stock on the tall, dense grasses of the Verde and to plant crops on the fertile river terraces. Understandably, the Yavapai vigorously resented this rude intrusion on their ancestral lands and launched raids and other forms of guerrilla warfare against the settlers.

Only after the U.S. military crushed native resistance did these first settlers dare venture into the surrounding mountains on prospecting trips. In June 1876 Morris Ruffner and his wife, Sarah, valley ranchers of modest means, filed claims on and around the outcrop noted by Espejo, dubbing one the "Eureka" and one the "Wade Hampton," after a hero of the Civil War. A few other ranchers filed claims as well. Ruffner insisted to his neighbors that someday his mine would be worth millions. With the nearest railhead in Abilene, Kansas, Ruffner's friends met his declarations with skepticism; they knew profits depended on cheap rail transportation from the mine site. Ruffner managed to convince brothers George and Angus McKinnon, Prescott shopkeepers, to take two-thirds interest in the claims in exchange for a grubstake. The partners, with pick, shovel and the most primitive of hoisting equipment, dug a forty-five foot shaft and drove a tunnel.

In 1882 Ruffner and the McKinnon brothers sold their mine. Profitable underground mining requires extensive capitalization in addition to modern transportation. The partners disclosed copper ore assaying high in gold and silver values but hauling this ore to the surface proved the least of their problems; the small grubstake provided by the McKinnons covered neither crippling freight charges to a railhead by ox team nor smelting costs at distant plants. Besides, the McKinnons did not share Ruffner's blind faith in the mine. They worried that the ore would pinch out, a reasonable assumption, considering that the majority of mining claims barely kept their owners in beans and bacon. A typical prospector vainly shoveled and sweated his way through the day and at night attended to aching muscles, severe blisters and perhaps a smashed finger or toe. Only in his dreams did he strike the motherlode. Holding majority interest, the McKinnons placed the claims on the market.

Among mining experts sent to investigate the property was Dr. James Douglas, co-inventor of the Hunt and Douglas process for refining low-grade copper and later, president of the Phelps Dodge Corporation of New York. Dr. Douglas travelled from the East to Arizona Territory in 1880 to solicit copper for custom smelting

*United Verde miners at old Jerome yard prepare to go underground in the 'cages' (1913). Courtesy Jerome Historical Society.*

*United Verde tractor shovel underground (1920s). Courtesy of Jerome Historical Society.*

at his small plant in Pennsylvania. Two Philadelphia capitalists, anxious to invest in Western mines, hired him to make a side trip to Ruffner's mine. Douglas recognized the ore's potential but advised his clients to reject the property because of transportation difficulties. One Philadelphian, Charles Lennig, disregarded Douglas' recommendation and purchased the Eureka claim.

By 1882, capitalists, both Eastern and Western, controlled the claims. Arizona Territorial governor, Frederick A. Tritle, appointed in 1882, engaged his own at-large expert in the mining field, one Frederick Thomas of California. Thomas had wide experience on the Comstock in Nevada. He met with Angus McKinnon in Prescott and the two rode over the mountains to the little shaft near the blue-green outcrop; after he examined the work in progress, Thomas urged Governor Tritle to take an option. Tritle, always a little short of cash, roped his friend, William Murray, into the deal; Murray, in Prescott for his health, had wealthy connections in the East. Tritle, Murray, and Thomas took a $500 option on the Wade Hampton claim, agreeing to pay Ruffner and the McKinnons $45,000 on expiration. To avoid future apex litigation over the property, the new owners bonded several more claims in the immediate vicinity of the Wade Hampton. Ruffner headed south, richer by $15,000, invested in a Gila River irrigation project, and lost the entire amount. He died in Phoenix in 1884, impoverished and disillusioned.

Tritle hit on the idea of drawing Eastern capital into the new partnership when he realized that in his enthusiasm to acquire the mine, he did not allow sufficient money to pay off Ruffner and the McKinnons. At his suggestion, partners Murray and Thomas sped back East in late 1882 to drum up some quick cash. In New York, Murray solicited funds from his uncle, Eugene Jerome, a banker and financier. Jerome conceded to his nephew the thrill of gambling at cards and at the horse track but held that the thought of risking money on a hole in the ground left him cold. Murray's petition, however, caught the fancy of Jerome's wife, a rich woman in her own right. She drew her sister into the scheme and the two raised $200,000 in development money, transferring it to the delighted Murray. With his wife's money irretrievably invested, Eugene Jerome, an able manager, took an active interest in the remote Arizona mine. Thomas later designated the infant camp sprouting up adjacent to the mine "Jerome", in honor of the family name. Neither Jerome nor his wife ever visited their namesake. Their nephew, Frederick Murray, did not care much for the rough little camp either; he doubled as both company agent and postmaster in Jerome, but being a Yale man, he preferred the bright lights and more civilized attractions of Prescott.

Additional investors included James A MacDonald, president of the Queen's Insurance Company of New York and Charles Lennig of Philadelphia, holder of the Eureka claim. On February 23, 1883,

*Work crew at surface of the United Verde mine, Jerome, turn-of-the-century. (KTVK-TV Collection)*

*William Andrews Clark, owner of the United Verde Mine. (KTVK-TV Collection)*

the new owners incorporated the United Verde Copper Company (UVCC) under New York laws with MacDonald as president, Lennig as vice president, and Jerome as secretary-treasurer. The Arizona partners, being only minor investors, were given charge of the more strenuous on-site development work.

By this time the Atlantic and Pacific Railway (later the Santa Fe) had reached Ash Fork, Arizona Territory, and the new mine owners built a sixty mile wagon road from the mine to the railhead. The company freighted in two small smelting furnaces by bull team over this rough road. Frederick Thomas made a fine show of superintending the UVCC, considering the primitive conditions he encountered. Surface ores ran high in gold and silver values -- so high that for a time, precious metals paid operating costs. Copper, for which a major market was just developing, amazed the mine managers with its purity and sold for fourteen cents per pound. Thomas reported an initial profit of $80,000, with which the company paid all debts and issued the first dividends.

In December 1884 company executives shut the mine down in response to plummeting copper prices and depletion of gold and silver in the rich surface ores. High freight charges and an inability (or reluctance) to invest heavily once again spelled disaster for hopeful investors. Governor Tritle, whose faith in the property matched that of its original locator, Morris Ruffner, leased the mine in the summer of 1887, but a dearth of capital vanquished him permanently. The UVCC unceremoniously cancelled his lease within two months. When mining experts pronounced the remaining ores to be "spotty" or irregular in quality, executives decided to sell.

Once again, the United Verde mine went on the market. Dr. James Douglas, who had investigated the property in 1880 and now worked for the Phelps Dodge Corporation as a mining expert, urged his employers to take an option. Now a front-leader in Southwestern copper mines, Phelps Dodge began negotiating, at which the UVCC promptly raised the asking price. Phelps Dodge just as promptly bowed out, leaving the field open to a most extraordinary man.

William Andrews Clark, copper king, industrial giant, Montana senator, and philanthropist, first noted UVCC ores in 1884 when he represented Montana Territory as commissioner to the New Orleans Exposition. As one of America's foremost mining men, well-versed in all technical and practical aspects of the craft, Clark recognized the Arizona ore samples as superb. At this time, Clark's Butte (Montana Territory) mines poured gratifying profits into the vaults of W.A. Clark and Brother, his privately-owned Butte bank and he toyed with the idea of expanding his empire. Clark kept his eye on the United Verde mine.

A few years later the Port Orford Copper Company of Verde Point, New Jersey, failed, becoming hugely indebted to Clark in the process. Poring over the company's books, Clark noticed that United Verde copper bullion, which the firm processed, assayed

*United Verde smelting works, Clarkdale, circa 1918. (KTVK-TV Collection)*

*United Verde smelting works, Jerome, circa 1903. (KTVK-TV Collection)*

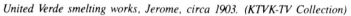

high in gold and silver content. This strengthened his interest. When Clark learned the mine was for sale, he summoned Joseph Giroux, superintendent of one of his Butte mines, and the two travelled to Jerome to look over the United Verde.

A small, wiry man with meticulously barbered whiskers and disorderly dark red hair, Clark paid painstaking attention to his elegantly subdued wardrobe. Yet never did he allow vanity to interfere with sound business principles. Thus, on his arrival in Jerome, Clark and Giroux both donned hardrock miners' overalls, boots, and hats and spent the major part of three weeks underground, carefully taking ore samples at twelve-inch intervals throughout the workings. Previous experts sampled carelessly at five-foot intervals and missed rich veins. Clark, a trained metallurgist, personally assayed the samples, confirming his earlier opinion that the United Verde contained bonanza ore. He took a $30,000 three-year option on the property at once.

Unlike most business tycoons of his time, Clark avoided mergers and partnerships, preferring, when necessary, to take on tractable family members as associates. His huge fortune, among the very largest in America, allowed him this luxury. True to form, Clark moved to gain personal control of the United Verde mine. Under the conditions of the option, Clark agreed to take one-half the mine's profits and turn the remainder over to company shareholders.

Clark's first ninety day run of ore yielded a $180,000 profit. His portion went toward the purchase of 160,000 shares of UVCC stock at one dollar per share and made him the company's largest stockholder. As profits soared under Clark's management, he continued buying shares until he controlled some ninety-five per-cent of UVCC stock. Only UVCC President James MacDonald refused to sell out, remaining the sole outside stockholder; his foresight made him a fortune.

From the beginning, Clark stoutly declined to disclose particulars of the mine's finances and underground development to the press or to government officials. It is difficult, then, to determine the exact purchase price of the mine; most historians estimate $200,000 to $300,000. The mine eventually netted him at least $50 million in profits. Clark turned down offers of as much as $90 million for the property from the world's great mining companies. To all offers he said simply, "The United Verde mine is not for sale at any price."

Clark considered the United Verde mine to be the jewel of his empire, a financial kingdom that included prosperous mines in nearly every Western state, Mexican rubber and coffee plantations, sugar factories in Southern California, and America's largest bronze factory in New York state. He built the San Pedro, Salt Lake, and Los Angeles Railroad early in the twentieth century, founding Las Vegas, Nevada, in the process. Grateful citizens named Clark County, Nevada, in his honor. Americans marveled as Clark spent

*Swimming Pool, Jerome, built by the United Verde Copper Company. (KTVK-TV Collection)*

*Clubhouse, Peck's Lake golf course, built by the United Verde Copper Company. (KTVK-TV Collection)*

extravagantly from a seemingly bottomless purse. He built fabulous houses in Butte, New York, and Santa Barbara, and travelled incessantly to Europe, collecting masterpieces of art for his renowned collection, now housed in the Corcoran Museum in Washington, D.C. His New York mansion, a prime example of the ostentatious tastes of the very rich of the period, contained four private galleries where Clark spent many hours contemplating his treasures. Indeed, as his holdings multiplied, Clark admitted that he could not list every one from memory.

Americans admired Clark as a self-made man. Born on a farm in Pennsylvania, Clark relocated with his family to Iowa to settle on more fertile land. Here he attended school and farmed with his father and brothers. He worked his way through Iowa Wesleyan University and accepted a teaching job in Missouri. In 1862 he followed a gold rush to Colorado and here obtained employment as a miner, learning the business from the ground up, so to speak. Clark's involvement in the Civil War is a mystery; he fought briefly with the Confederate Army in Missouri and may have been wounded. He followed another gold rush to Bannack (Montana Territory) in 1863 and filed a claim at nearby Horse Prairie. In his first season on the placers, he washed out $3,000 in gold, having entered Bannack with five dollars in Colorado gold dust in his poke.

Unlike most young men in frontier camps, Clark refrained from spending his money on women, whiskey, and gambling over the cold winter, though he appreciated all three. Instead, in the late autumn of 1863, he rode south to Salt Lake City where he invested in dozens of eggs, an item his fellow miners craved. He freighted the eggs back to Bannack through a severe blizzard and eager miners snatched them up at three dollars per dozen. Ambition and initiative characterized Clark's career from this time; he had an exceptional knack for merchandising, banking, and generally being in the right place at the right time. His early merchandising efforts earned him the nickname "Baking Powder" Bill, a sobriquet he soon outgrew. Instrumental in the development of Butte, one of the world's great mining centers, Clark made his home and fortune there and always claimed Montana as his state of residence.

Throughout a stellar and honorable business career, Clark practiced a typical but shrewd philanthropy. He believed a "free" ride eventually crippled able-bodied adults but held that working men and women deserved comfortable housing, pleasant and wholesome leisure activities, fair wages, and safe working conditions. From the Paul Clark Home for Orphans and the Columbia Gardens ( a deluxe resort for the workingman) in Butte to the model town of Clarkdale in Arizona; from the Mary Andrews Clark Home for Working Women in Los Angeles to the Katherine Stauffer Clark Kindergarten in New York, Clark used the finest building materials and the most modern equipment. He incorporated his philanthropic principles into solid brick structures and tranquil green retreats.

The ingenious and sometimes unscrupulous role William Andrews Clark played in Montana's War of the Copper Kings eclipsed an otherwise honorable political career. In this fierce struggle for control of Montana's mineral resources, Clark played the lone wolf against corporate giants like the Amalgamated Copper Company, a piratical brainchild of Standard Oil executives. Clark took up the weapons of his enemies: money, a controlled press, and carefully orchestrated lawsuits. With these and his huge popularity in Montana, he stormed his way into the U.S. Senate against all odds and held the corporate octopus at bay in Butte for years.

In Butte, Clark's enemies pointed to his benevolence and projects to better his employees' lives and working conditions as inducements to garner votes in his bids for the Senate. Personal political considerations did not motivate Clark in Jerome, though he occasionally involved himself in Arizona politics for business reasons. His career in the Jerome district provides a far more accurate measure of the man than his actions in Montana.

Clark's development of the United Verde mine demonstrates his acute business sense. When he acquired control, Jerome clung to the mountain near the mine, a sorry jumble of rickety cabins, canvas tents, and a store or two; in ten years the United Verde was Arizona's top copper producer. The original smelting works consisted of Tritle's two water jacket furnaces and little more, while most of the mine's underground workings had barely penetrated the surface ore. Clark judged it a promising property but he could not be certain he had a bonanza on his hands. Previous UVCC capitalists wavered when it came to heavy investing in the property, especially in the area of modern transportation, the mine's biggest problem. Clark, on the other hand, staked much of his burgeoning fortune on the chance that he owned a big producer.

Six years of intense development work followed; money poured into the mine and copper flowed out. Clark's most ambitious project was the construction of a twenty-seven mile-long narrow-gauge railway, the United Verde and Pacific, completed in 1895, which zig-zagged its way from the mine over the mountains to connect with the new Santa Fe line at Jerome Junction, between Ash Fork and Phoenix. By this time, hardrock miners had drilled and blasted their way underground to a depth of five hundred feet. Veteran miners daily exposed an orebody that waxed in size and richness until it appeared to have no limit. Assay and progress reports elated Clark, as well they might, for deep under the booming camp of five hundred rested the largest deposit of high-grade pyritic copper ever discovered in the United States and one of the most extensive in the world.

As news of Clark's discovery circulated, miners, prospectors, and those who pocketed their earnings converged on the camp. A cosmopolitan population, typical of boom towns, thronged Jerome's boardwalks and rutted streets. From boarding houses and saloons jammed with miners there issued the clamor of a dozen languages. Excitement reigned in old Jerome but, as in most camps, beauty and gracious living sat below the salt. Prospect holes scarred the mountains and urban planning was unknown. To remove unwanted sulphur from the ore before transfer to Clark's new smelter, heaps of roasting ore smouldered at the mouth of every tunnel. The sulphur-laden smoke, a common sight in camps at the time, stung the eyes, caused paroxysms of coughing, and killed every trace of vegetation in town. Mules hauled the ore to the smelter, located for topographical reasons directly atop the underground workings. At the smelter, modern in every respect, workers produced a constant stream of gleaming copper bullion and a smaller amount of gold and silver. Mining experts and the few visitors allowed in the smelter remarked on the top-of-the-line machinery and equipment Clark installed, and the rigid safety measures he required his men to follow on pain of dismissal.

Before the turn of the century, Clark shipped sixty-million pounds per year of copper bullion from Jerome and his personal profits from the property exceeded ten million dollars. United Verde profits plus millions more generated by his far-flung interests made Clark one of America's richest men; some "experts" in the field of estimating other peoples' fortunes declared that Clark's hidden wealth, in the form of buried ores in his many mines, made him far richer than John D. Rockefeller, then deemed America's wealthiest citizen.

Barring a few brief shutdowns, the UVCC operated steadily over the years. Clark conferred routine management of the company on his sons, Charles and William, Jr. Both executed their duties admirably but always looked to their father for guidance. Until his death in 1925, Clark made all major decisions. In 1912, the senior Clark announced a grandiose project, the biggest he ever undertook. An underground fire in the main orebody, ignited by the friction of a cave-in in 1894, put the smelter and surface works in danger of collapse. Slowly-burning timbers under the smelter caused the ground to give and workmen continually shored up loose foundations. Clark spent heavily to extinguish the fire but to no avail. Perhaps the man could not move the mountain but he could move the smelter.

In 1910 Clark bought a number of ranches in the Verde Valley below Jerome, along with water rights. Here he would build not only a new reduction works, but a model town to attract and hold stable family men who would, he hoped, become loyal and steady employees. He set the best mining engineers and architects to work and by the summer of 1913, construction crews filled the once peaceful valley, stirring up great clouds of dust and cursing their mules.

Railroad men laid out tracks for three lines: the Verde Valley Railway, a thirty-eight mile broad-gauge running from the townsite

*James Douglas, Jr., owner of the Little Daisy Mine. (KTVK-TV Collection)*

to Drake on the Santa Fe line; the Verde Tunnel and Smelter Railway (VT&S), an eleven- mile road between the mine and townsite which transported ore and passengers; and the electric Hopewell Tunnel Railway which hauled ore through the 7200-foot long Hopewell Tunnel at the 1000-foot level of the mine to connect with the VT&S line. Clark's new brick plant near the townsite turned out thousands of bricks each day to be used for the smelter buildings and town. He required all construction, including the business district to conform to unusually high standards.

Clark's Upper Verde Public Utilities Company (UVPU), an umbrella organization which provided water, light, and power for Jerome, administered and owned Clarkdale. From garbage crew to police department, Clark and his managers controlled the town through the UVPU. An enlightened concern for employee welfare somewhat offset this circumscribing paternalism.

Brick houses (patio-style in the Hispanic section) boasted maple floors, screened sleeping porches, indoor plumbing, electricity, and free water each summer for lawns and gardens. Employees were offered modern electric ranges at cost; Clarkdale had more of these per capita than any town in America. Broad streets surrounded a spacious central plaza, planted in grass, trees, and shrubs; Clark ordered that no "Keep Off the Grass" signs be posted. After hours, employees and their families might stroll to the clubhouse and check out a library book, go for a swim, play a game of tennis, attend a hotly-contested baseball game with Jerome or play a round of golf; the UVCC donated first-class accommodations for all these activities. A mining town with no saloon is unthinkable; Clark allowed three to operate but forbade a red-light district.

Clark's will stipulated a $100,000 endowment for the construction of a new clubhouse. This superb example of Spanish-style architecture, embellished with copper, housed a bowling alley, billiard room, auditorium, lounges and cardrooms for men and women, soda fountain, and library -- most facilities were free of charge for employees and families. Clark's heirs spared no effort to equip the clubhouse with the finest furnishings. Clark spent at least six million dollars over the years on Clarkdale.

As company officials fired up the new smelter in May, 1915, and Clarkdale assumed the air of a model town, a new Jerome mine owner dazzled the mining world. James Stuart Douglas came to Jerome in 1912 to look over the Little Daisy mine, owned by the United Verde Extension Company (UVX). Many called him "Rawhide," not for any trait of character but for a rawhide device he concocted in Mexico to save wear on mining machinery. "Rawhide" suited him though; Douglas was a block of a man, with a disarming smile that tempered somewhat rugged features. His mercurial temperament intimidated some, yet many remarked on his generosity and sense of fair play. His father, Dr. James Douglas, famous in mining circles, presided over the Phelps Dodge

*Vertical stope drilling underground - United Verde (1925). Jerome Historical Society.*

*Leyner on a tripod - United Verde branch of Phelps Dodge Mining Co. (1941). Courtesy of Jerome Historical Society.*

Corporation for many years and devoted his later years to good works. Dr. Douglas had inspected the United Verde mine for investors twice -- once in 1881 for the Philadelphia investors and again in 1888 for Phelps Dodge. He showed less enthusiasm for the Jerome district than for the copper districts to the south.

If Dr. Douglas made no great splash in Jerome, his son certainly did. "Rawhide" James Douglas, born in Quebec in 1868, like Clark, embodied that unrestrained boldness, focused ambition, and strong independence that characterized so many prosperous nineteenth-century businessmen. In the West, these qualities almost always guaranteed success (or a jail term). Young Douglas did not gravitate at once to mining; it had ruined his grandfather financially and frustrated his father for years. Instead, Douglas, an asthmatic, chose at age seventeen to homestead, alone, on Manitoba's Red River. He farmed, but not well, and supplemented his income freighting supplies for the Canadian National Railway, then under construction.

Five years later, in 1890, Douglas moved on to Arizona Territory where he raised strawberries in Cochise County, location of Phelps Dodge's most productive copper mines. Farming defeated him a second time and forced Douglas, a proud young man, to make use of his father's influence to gain employment. The Phelps Dodge Corporation took him on as an assayer in Bisbee and a year later sent him to Prescott in the same capacity at the company's Big Bug, Senator, and Commercial mines. Company officials quickly recognized young Douglas' managerial talents and promoted him to superintendent of the Prescott properties where he remained until 1900. During this time, he became familiar with the Jerome district.

From 1900-1913 Douglas supervised Phelps Dodge's Picacho and Canannea mines in Sonora, Mexico, where he increased production by cutting expenses and modernizing mining methods. Occasionally he ran afoul of the local populace in his efforts to economize and once had to flee the country for three days when his miners walked off the job and threatened to ride him out of town on a burro. Blame for the strike cannot be placed entirely on Douglas; all of Mexico seethed with revolution at the time. Douglas' thrifty ways ended his association with Phelps Dodge when he made unwelcome attempts to cut expenses at company headquarters in New York. When executives took offense at what they perceived as a young upstart's impertinence, he resigned.

When Douglas came to Jerome in 1912, he had found his niche in mining, banking, and promotion. He still worked for Phelps Dodge and divided his time between Mexico and the American border town of Douglas which he founded and named for his father. He grew wealthy in real estate speculation and established the banks of Bisbee and Douglas. Like Clark, Douglas diversified, having many interests outside mining.

In Jerome, Douglas examined the Little Daisy mine, property

of the UVX Company. J.J. Fisher, a surveyor, located the Little Daisy claim in 1899 in the maze of claims in and about Jerome; prospectors overlooked this tiny fraction of ground in the rush to lay claim to the mountain in the wake of Clark's great success. Fisher convinced L.E. Whichner, a Boston capitalist who owned claims in Jerome, to back the sinking of a shaft. Whichner halted the flow of capital in 1901 because of poor ore showings. In 1902, though, Whichner regained his enthusiasm and acquired four claims adjoining the Little Daisy. Whichner, Fisher, and a few others merged interests, organizing the United Verde Extension Company the same year. With depth the quality of ore improved. Whichner, in need of more capital, joined forces with Douglas in 1912.

The Little Daisy came to Douglas' notice through Major A. J. Pickerell, a UVX stockholder with great faith in the mine and a friend of Douglas. In 1911 the Major urged Douglas to evaluate the Little Daisy, hoping he would kick in some working capital. Douglas liked what he saw and tried to interest Phelps Dodge in a partnership option. For a second time, the company turned down a stake in Jerome, ostensibly over a problem with title to the mine but more probably because Phelps Dodge feared apex litigation with Clark, a veteran of many apex suits in Butte. Pickerell tried a new tack; he urged Douglas to undertake the option himself. Douglas hired the famous mining geologist, Ira Joralemon, to make a final report before leaping in. Joralemon told Douglas the odds were good on a money-making prospect. Douglas leapt.

At this point in his career, Douglas had made the acquaintance of a number of wealthy capitalists and expert mining men. He did not have the resources to tackle the Little Daisy venture alone so appealed to these men. George E. Tener of Pittsburgh, a director of Jerome's Calumet and Arizona Company, agreed at once to invest. Tener and Douglas took an option on shares then fired off letters to prospective investors.

Among those who bought in were Chester Congdon and James Hoatson, associates of Tener; Henry Hoveland of Live Oaks (Arizona) Development; Arthur James of Phelps Dodge; and John D. Ryan, president of Amalgamated Copper Company of Butte. Whichner, the previous owner, sat on the board of directors. The inclusion of Ryan among the UVX stockholders jolted Clark, who possessed no greater enemy than Amalgamated, which after years of struggle, forced a sell-out of his Butte copper properties in 1910.

Clark naturally took an interest in UVX progress. He noted the thousands of dollars that went into development and the thousands more that company president, Douglas, requested from share-holders. For two years, a small force of hardrock men probed Little Daisy ground and Douglas assured the people of Jerome that a great copper deposit would be found. The first big ore strike came in December, 1914, when Little Daisy miners cut into an immense vein of 45 per-cent copper ore. It is easy to imagine

Clark, in the privacy of his New York offices, grimly bemoaning the discovery of bonanza ore right under his nose; especially so, because originally the Little Daisy and the United Verde ore bodies were one. An ancient geological accident separated a sizeable chunk from the main body.

Clark's own discovery of ore attracted many lesser companies to the mountains around Jerome, all intent on striking it rich. These organizations invested heavily in their claims from 1915 on, but not one approached the wealth of the United Verde. By the time of Douglas' discovery, geologists proved that only one deposit of high-grade copper existed in the district. Millions of years before, a fault cut through the top of this pipe-shaped structure, slicing off the top, which then slid off and buried itself somewhere in the vicinity. Mining men knew of the fault and the possibility of more bonanza ore; Douglas took a calculated risk that he owned the missing section and won.

Dividend payments from Jerome's two great mines tell the story; the Little Daisy yielded $52 million in dividends, split by a number of shareholders, before final shutdown in 1937; the United Verde paid several million before 1900, at least $60 million between 1900-1927, and millions more to Clark's heirs. A further indication of wealth buried beneath the surface of the United Verde is that Phelps Dodge paid over $10 million to the heirs for the property in the midst of the Great Depression, and realized a further profit of some $40 million before final shutdown in 1953.

Clark and Douglas never became implacable rivals. Though embroiled in litigation between 1916-1922 over which company owned title to disputed mining stocks, both men put aside their differences in 1917 to form a mine owners protective association with a view to putting down labor unrest, a rarity in the district. Profit always took precedence for both men. Political differences never developed; as Democrats and mine owners, both had a vested interest in pro-company legislation and cooperated to that end. Clark's sons followed the lead of their father and lived peacefully with Douglas.

The Jerome district boomed through World War I. Clark, now in his seventies, made annual inspection trips to Jerome and Clarkdale but spent most of his time in New York. Douglas began building a fine mansion in Jerome near the Little Daisy and when the Great War broke out, volunteered his services. The Red Cross accepted his offer and gave him charge of all the organization's warehouses in France. He became a lover of all things French during his stay, another trait he shared with Clark.

After the war, Douglas built his own smelter and support city, naming it after his new friend, Premier Georges Clemenceau of France. The Premier made Douglas a Chevalier of the Legion of Honor in 1927 for his Red Cross work. Douglas did not establish Clemenceau on nearly so grand a scale as Clarkdale, but he built it with a degree of genuine concern for the well-being of his employees. Unlike Clark, Douglas had balky stockholders to contend with when making improvements or attending to employee welfare. Douglas built the handsome and spacious Little Daisy Hotel near the mine to house his men, and a modern company hospital to care for their medical needs.

Clark and Douglas both shut down their mines in 1921 in response to a nation-wide post-war slump. As America recovered, so did Jerome; through the remainder of the twenties, the district's smokestacks emitted choking white smoke day and night, skips roared up and down mine shafts, mine sirens shrieked, long trains of ore cars clacked along to smelter, and the streets of Jerome, Clarkdale, and Clemenceau swarmed with three shifts of miners and smeltermen. Only Clark's death in 1925, of pneumonia, at age eighty-seven, caused activity at the UVCC to cease; all operations stopped for a day in his memory. His sons effected a smooth transition and the good times continued until the Great Depression.

The UVCC shut down in the early years of the Depression, partly in response to low copper prices but also because both Clark's sons and his grandson, Tertius, heir apparent to the Clark empire, died. His daughters, Mary and Katherine, inherited, but sold out to Phelps Dodge in 1935. The Little Daisy played out in 1938, and James Douglas, in a fit of pique over Roosevelt's New Deal Program, renewed his Canadian citizenship, making his home in Montreal until his death in 1949 at eighty years of age. As long as he lived, Douglas returned regularly to Jerome to visit old haunts.

William Andrews Clark and James "Rawhide" Douglas are long dead, but visitors to Jerome see everywhere evidence of the King and the Crown Prince of Copper. Well worth a side trip, Clarkdale itself is a monument to Clark, a man who succeeded brilliantly in the material building of the West during a time when most Americans considered progress and growth to be nothing less than humanity's highest goal. Clark built many of Jerome's historic buildings; his influence permeates the town. Douglas stamped his image over a more limited area, perhaps, but his presence remains strong. His elegant mansion is now headquarters for the Jerome State Historic Park, a fine museum and park devoted to Jerome's mining history. Clemenceau is gone but the skeleton of the Little Daisy Hotel remains, as does the site of the fabulous Little Daisy Mine.

While Jerome stands, Clark and Douglas live, symbols of a past era, one in which anything was possible, when remarkable men wrested fame and fortune from the earth.

*Early prospectors in Jerome. (KTVK-TV Collection)*

Jeanette Rodda is a professional historian specializing in environmental and labor history. She is a native of Butte Montana and currently resides in Flagstaff, Arizona.

# JEROME'S BILLION DOLLAR BOOM DOLLAR BOOM BUSTLE AND BUST

*1898 To The Present*

*By Nancy R. Smith*

side from Fort Verde and the occasional ranch house, prospectors in the Black Hills of Arizona only had their burros, dogs and assorted animals for companionship. After the mining camp of Jerome became established, saloons and gambling resorts became favorite places of entertainment and socializing for these solitary hunters of fortune.

One day the old prospector known as Rim Rock, meandered into the saloon of Joe Seegar. Charlie Brown, an apprentice foundry worker for the United Verde, recalls the event in his HISTORY OF JEROME:

*"Rim's poke holds a medium sized fortune in placer gold." Of course Joe was anxious to find out where Rim panned it. With seven free drinks under his sunburned belly skin, he loosened up -- I heard the whole yarn. 'One night there was a hell of a wind storm blew up and I filled my pockets with rocks to keep from blowin' away. Didn't do any good. Next morning I was cleanin' out my pockets, and durned if it wasn't mostly placer gold. I musta got blowed more than twenty miles. I was so shook up, I laid mostly dead for three days, when my dog Dusty come leadin' the burro into camp. Dusty had a fresh killed rabbit in his mouth. The burro had the canteen in his pack an' it was full. That was three months ago, and I've been looking for the place where I camped ever since. I had to come in for grub, and I'm goin' right back to look some more.' Whiskey makes a pretty good lie detector, so Joe poured old Rim seven more drinks. When old Rim came to, he didn't even know his name or where he was. [Joe] took the price of the drinks from Rim's poke. Where the gold came from remains a mystery to this day. Old Rim with his dog Dusty, and his burro disappeared and has never come back to Jerome, or any other place. Old Timers think he is somewhere in the mountains still looking for the place from where he was blown. Some folks think old Rim was lyin' about not knowing who he was when he came to. Joe Seeger thinks different, he declared that fourteen drinks of the booze he gave old Rim would make a mummy talk. He ought to know!"*

In those days, hard-rock miners could be a loose and wild bunch. They needed a place to unwind, and, if possible, with understanding women. Mr. Brown tells of such a place located in Walnut, aka Deception Gulch:

*"Below the Hog-back ridge of rocks there was a lovely little gulch. Trees and bushes and grass throve there. Sulfur fumes never reached its verduned slopes. It was sparsely settled, being without a road, and much too far for walking into town up the rocky paths. It was called Deception gulch. No one knew why. Its waters were cool, clear, and scant. Its slopes were ever green and blooming. After the war with Spain and "Remember the Main!" An enterprising man had saved his money made during the war, and built a road of fair grades to reach its depths. There he constructed a saloon and dance hall. It soon became the rendezvous for our wilder spirited youths, both men and girls. A mechanical piano was operated by a man who knew how to pedal it. Fist fights between ten cent dances were common. It reached its nadir of rowdyism when two contenders for a little Mexican girl's snuggles went outside to win or lose. A stalwart named Elmer, bit off his rival's ear. He won and spit out the morsel, and snuggled his sweetie-pie. The law which had kept hands off hitherto, decided things were getting out of hand at the Dewey Cafe. By popular acclaim the gulch got a new name CANNIBAL GULCH. Teeth and fingers had been lost in previous fights, but somehow, an ear struck the popular fancy as beyond fair fighting."*

Since the ore body appeared capable of producing gold, silver and copper for an indeterminate number of years, the business men and women invested their money and energy into buildings which would last. One of the things they felt necessary to help insure their investments was incorporation as a town in the Territory of Arizona. This would allow tax monies to stay in the town and not go to be spent for roads, fire systems and other necessities somewhere else. As has been recorded many times, in the early days of tents and flimsy wood structures, the fire demon swept through major parts of Jerome at least 4 times in less than 12 years. Incorporation could lead to laws to prohibit wooden structures within the main commercial area. It would also allow the town to form a Jerome Volunteer Fire Department, and equip it to adequately fight fires.

The Town of Jerome was approved by the Yavapai County Board of Supervisors on March 8, 1899. The Common Council was set up, and William M. Munds, owner of the Jerome Meat Market, became Mayor. This Council established the government and instituted the first ordinances directed at the health and safety of the 5000 plus citizens reported to be in and around Jerome. Civic responsibility and duty became the major spare-time activity of many of the men. But not all of men of the town!

The Jerome Volunteer Fire Department organized their Chemical Company #1 on July 27, 1899. Tom Campbell, assistant Post Master (and later Governor of Arizona) was elected Chief, and Tom Page became Assistant Chief. On August 1st a Hose company was to be organized. There were eventually 3 companies in the Fire Department: Pronto Chemical, Victor Hose and Miller Hose. The

*Jerome Volunteer Fire Department hose company racing team, c. 1910*

*Holiday on Main Street, c. 1910*

*United Verde's company hill and society rows, c. 1900*

fire hose companies formed teams and competed amongst themselves and against other towns. Prescott was a favorite opponent. This was a popular racing event, especially on the Fourth of July.

Prior to the Chemical Company's formation, the Town had a fund-raising dance to buy a chemical engine for the city. The community was good for fund-raisers and loved to have dances. The Jerome band even had a ball to raise money for their instruments! It has been said that the most popular activity in this town throughout the years has been to drink beer and dance. The Fashion Saloon itself sold 150 kegs in 17 days one summer!

The Fire Department's Annual Ball, traditionally held around the 21st of February, was an excellent fund-raiser, and was often considered the social event of the season. The firemen had dress uniforms, maroon and silver and worn especially at the gala affair. Those men who did not wear uniforms wore evening clothes and gloves. The women got new dresses for the event and they danced with everyone.

Other distractions, designed to make Life more than just work, were the up-town saloons, such as the Fashion, the Senate, Shea's place, and the Manhattan. Intoxicants, card and board games, and light entertaiment were provided. In 1903 Jerome was able to boast having the "Largest and Most Complete Establishment of Its Kind in the Southwest, If Not On the Continent." The Fashion Saloon, now housing the Jerome Historical Society's Mine Museum, advertised its new addition. The JEROME MINING NEWS printed the story, from which the following excerpts are taken:

*"This immense establishment now occupies a building with a frontage of 50 feet and a depth of 180 feet, with four floors . . . nearly one-half acre of floor spaces on which to accommodate their business. Jerome B. Hoover and Arthur Cordiner, the owners of this establishment, came to Jerome 8 years ago, and purchased what was known as the Stoney lot and a frame building located thereon, being what was and is now conceded to be the best business location in the then camp and now city of Jerome. They made many improvements in the old building, and carried on a successful business there until Sept 11, 1898, when the great fire of that date destroyed their building and its contents, they saving only the stock of goods stored in a fire proof cellar on the hillside.."*

Fire struck again on May 19, 1899.

*"It was then that the business world appreciated that their motto, 'We Never Sleep,' carried on their stationary, was not meaningless, for before the fire had completed its work of destruction the wires were carrying messages ordering supplies with which to replace the loss, and within 18 months from the date of the fire the mortgage had been released . . ."*
*The upper floor of the old Fashion is occupied by a bar, gambling tables, a business" office in the front and private card and social rooms in the rear . . . A broad flight of stairs lead from this room to the German beer and lunch room below. "The new addition to The Fashion (now occupied by Paul and Jerry's Saloon) is entered either from the main street or through a large archway cut through the south wall of the concrete*

*building...The room has been entirely renovated and refurnished. The bar in this room is a half circle, the only one of its kind in the territory, and is of polished oak, the back bar being an original and elegant design...The basement in this part of the house is well lighted and has been fitted for use as a bowling alley...In the house there are 11 games of chance in operation, including faro, craps, roulette, monte, stud poker and a Chinese lottery...To successfully carry on this business over 30 people are employed, the payroll amounting to considerably over $50,000 per year."*

News of sporting events and politics were communicated by wire to the Fashion and interested patrons. The length of the lease on the addition, the old Senate saloon, was 5 years with an option for renewal. The temperature of the town, the territory and soon the nation was to turn cold to gambling, booze and women in saloons. The Fashion never picked up the option after gambling became illegal in Jerome in 1906.

Most of the women of Jerome did not frequent such places. Those who did were usually singers, musicians and entertainers. Not to be confused with the "bad girls" who worked the brothels and back streets, these women were educated, refined, stylish, and cultured. They often married leading men of the community. The Company doctor, Dr. Charles Woods, married a French violinist, an ex-entertainer in a saloon. She also gave children of the community music lessons. At that time it was an insult for a woman of the "elite" to go out and get a job -- but singing was alright. Before she arrived in Jerome, the wife of one of the Company's Bosses heard that the only women in Jerome after the turn of the century were ex-saloon entertainers. She often went to card parties and socials wondering which of the ladies used to work in a saloon. The first "proper" invitation she received after coming to Jerome was engraved, and from the doctor's wife!

After the opening of the United Verde & Pacific Railway in 1894, the population quickly grew to include the wives and families of the Company Bosses and the "common" miners. The little narrow gauge ran six trains daily for the most part. People and goods traveled in and out of Jerome. Boarding and rooming houses were everywhere. The United Verde provided limited housing for its employees and their families. Downhill from the mine plant and smelter were wooden Queen Anne style houses for the Bosses. In later years this area was called Company Hill or Society Row.

Here the "Elite" lived. That is, those who did not own their own houses. The men held such jobs as General Manager, Chief Timekeeper, Chief Engineer, Underground Construction Foreman, and Smelter Superintendent. The women raised their children, managed the household, and often the servants, and involved themselves in church and other social activities.

In-house help was not just for those of the Company Hill. Other families were used to having help do household chores also. The nationalities of the servants varied. Glenellen Minty Ewell recalls Japanese and Chinese cooks. She also recalls how hard it could be to get help to stay. It seems they either could not stand the life in Jerome, or they got married and took care of their own houses, possibly taking in laundry.

One of Glenellen's most vivid memories was of Susie, the local Apache Indian woman who worked for the Minty family on the Hill. Susie lived on the Hogback where there was a little Apache camp of 3 or 4 wigwams. Glenellen relates:

*"She was quite a character. She worked for us at times, her niece Maggie too. What a beautiful pianist she was! she was well educated at Carlyle Indian school. There she sat in her bright calicos at our Steinway piano, fingers rippling over the keys, playing a beautiful piece of music! This "wild" Apache!...Susie's husband was John Ketchum. He was one of General Crook's Scouts. 'All Indian Squaws wore bright colored skirts, quite full, and under this were 3 or 4 full petticoats. I watched Susie disrobe once when she was to mop our kitchen. These garments neatly folded. Her black under slip was knee length; wore heavy black stockings. (Her) garments peeking through black slip were light color. She seemed to use several large safety pins! I still wonder how they kept so clean! Susie was a good worker and wouldn't use a mop -- floors weren't clean unless scrubbed. There were no gadgets then, like vacuum, etc. Just a broom; carpet sweepers came in later."*

It has been said that the social standing of a person was established by where on Cleopatra Hill she lived. This is not necessarily so, as there were fine people living everywhere on the hill. There were, however, different neighborhoods. Company Hill or the Society Rows have been mentioned. South of that area high on Cleopatra was another privately-owned residential area. Here there were a number of multi-family homes, with residents of many different nationalities and professions. The southern residential areas were mostly known by the names of the mining claims they were on: Copper Chief, 16 to 1, Mountain View, and the Florencia. The "Hogbacks" were on the "arm" extending toward the valley. Sturdy concrete and brick houses were built on the Lower Hogback (Hampshire Ave.) by the United Verde Extension mining company for their geologists, warehouse foremen, doctors, comptrollers and such. The wives here also tended to have in-house help, play bridge, tennis, and socialize as much as possible.

The Mexican and/or Spanish people lived together in separate neighborhoods. They were known as El Palomar (below the Hotel Jerome), El Barrio Chicano (below the main commercial district), El Verde (downhill from the Powderbox Church), El Golcho (primarily the upper Gulch Road area known Blue Bend), and La Daisy (the town by the Douglas Mansion created for their workers). Family and church were the main focuses of social activites in these neighborhoods. In isolated communities such as Jerome, people must create their own entertainment when they do not wish to take

*Jerome Opera Company presents "The Mikado," Feb. 27, 1906*

*Apache Indian house servant, c. 1905*

*The elite ladies socialize c. 1910*

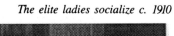

advantage of commercial ventures. Before the fires at the turn of the century there had been an Opera House located on the south edge of the commercial district. A finer one was to come.

The T.F. Miller Company, a mercantile store, was originally located in Jerome on the mine road above the Congregational church. Miller, a relative of William Clark, wanted to relocate closer to the commercial district and the growing residential areas. In 1898 a four story brick structure was started. It opened in 1899, and was to house not only the largest mercantile company in town, but also places for businesses on the ground level, a floor for lodge rooms, and a floor large enough for an Opera House facility, complete with stage. The Jerome newspaper of December 11, 1899, announced:

*"The new Jerome Opera House will be formally opened next Tuesday and Wednesday evenings December 19 and 20, by America's greatest romantic actor, Paul Gilmore. Manager (Walter) Miller is to be congratulated upon securing such a first-class performance for his opening. Mr. Gilmore will produce Dumas' Immortal Romance, "The Musketeers" on Tuesday evening, and "Don Caesar" on Wednesday evening." "McCarty's Mishaps" was scheduled as the next production, and was billed as the "funniest farce comedy ever written." Another period favorite was the temperance play "Ten Nights in a Barroom."*

Later talented local people formed the Jerome Opera Company, performing classics in full costume. The February 27, 1906 program for "The Mikado" gave the following officers and performers of the community: Mrs. C.A. Minty, musical director; R.A. Armstrong, business manager; A.H. Dawson, secretary-treasurer; honorary members Gen. & Mrs. R.H.G. Minty, Rev. & Mrs. H.G. Miller; performers Mrs. L.E. Arnott, Miss Vesta Docker, Misses Faull, Dorland, Fagerland, Johnson and Goodwin, Mrs. A.H. Lyons, Mr. and Mrs. C.V. Brockway, Mr. and Mrs. Mrs. W.C. Miller, E. Brockway, C. Havelin, J.J. Kuder, W.S. Owen, Dr. J.W. Coleman, C.V. Harris, T. Merrill, and Mr. J. Sharp. Mrs. Minty taught vocal and music to serious students, as well as performing warm duets with her husband for their family and friends.

The Opera House facility provided a place for masquerade balls, grand dances for all groups including the annual ball of the Fire Department, and dances for all the societies. Fairs were held to raise funds for churches and charities. And, of course, Jerome was on the Southwestern theater circuit which provided the finest professional performers available to small, isolated communities.

Charlie Brown recalls:

*"One time when a Stock Company was giving a play in the Company Store hall, the biggest laugh to ever greet an actor's lines, occured when the Tough Moll was found weeping in her sordid bedroom by her heartless 'Man'. I see him yet! He came into the room with his hat on the back of his head, hands in his jacket pockets, shut the door with his rump, and decisively sneered. 'Well! Water - front Mag crying?' At that sublime*

*moment, just outside the open window, a burro raised his voice in lamentation of his cruel fate. Oh! It might have been his love-call. One event like that in a life time should be enough for any one. Two such, would be utterly incredible. What could the sobbing voice of a fallen woman do against the He-haw of a melancholy jack-ass.''*

An Arizona Canary! That is another name for the four legged garbage disposals left to wander nightly on the streets and through the yards of Jerome. Their owners, usually wood haulers, would round them up in the morning, well fed, and put them to another day's work. In later years the children would commandeer a burro for a ride to school or to a friend's house.

A Ladies' Social Union was formed by the women of the "Elite." Its objective was sociability. Calling on each other, attired in hobble skirts, gloves and leaving calling cards, became hard going considering the terrain in the upper part of town. It was decided to meet twice a month in particular homes. Later the gatherings were held at the Congregational church.

The Company Hill wives met often for card games such as 500, bridge and casino. Since the Victorian living room of the Company house was small, they often had to take down the beds, moving them outside with other extraneous furniture to make room for the 4 or 5 tables necessary for the afternoon's games. If and when the weather changed, there was a scurry to get the beds back inside.

Churches provided another location for social activities and fulfilled the need of religion in the now booming mining camp. The Baptists built the church later sold to the Congregationalists. The Catholics had their first edifice above Company Hill, but it burned in the 1898 fire. They soon built a brick church, the Church of the Holy Family, which still stands above town on the old mine road.

The Methodists chose another part of the hill on which to build their sanctuary. In 1899 they provided a Protestant church for the south side of Jerome, in another residential area. The congregation grew, needing a new building 20 years later. Of the various groups who worshiped in Jerome, the Methodist have maintained services to this date.

At first there were few Episcopalians in town. The Congregationalist church was the closer of the two Protestant churches to the homes of these families so they attended services there. In early 1898 General R.H.G. Minty, ex-Civil war leader and Auditor for the narrow gauge railway, started reading services to a group who called themselves the Christ Church. The next year a more "official" church was organized by the Bishop of Arizona. In later years they bought the old church from the Congregationalists. Still later, they built a fine edifice which remains today above the Town Park.

On Sunday afternoons it was customary to pack a picnic lunch and go for a walk on one of the many well-worn trails around

Jerome. A favorite was the hike up Hull's Canyon to Hull's mine, about 3 miles. On a particulary good day, the walk could continue on to Walnut Springs, meeting neighbors and friends there and along the way. Young people adventurously walked the tracks of the narrow gauge or climbed the giant rocks around the Gulch. Hiking was commonplace since automobiles, introduced to Jerome in 1903, were not. Motorcycles were seen more often on the narrow trails. Groups of cyclists would go for an outing, occasionally ending up in Camp Verde or the Montezuma Castle area.

Mercantile stores delivered groceries, which made life easier for many ladies trapped in period clothing. The order could be phoned in since telephones came to Jerome in 1899. Johnny Lyons' market used horses, and the T.F. Miller Company used mules and some saddle horses. The groceries were held in two large baskets, one on each side of the animal. A small child could fit into the 3'x2'x2' and balance an uneven load of goods. Light wagons were used on the wider roads.

The Jerome Gun Club was established, not only to provide a group to go hunting with, but to also provide a club where men could practice shooting clay pigeons. The shooting range was located across lower Main Street from the Methodist church, overlooking Bitter Creek Gulch. This group competed with ones from other towns. In 1899, a Thanksgiving Turkey shoot was held out at Jerome Junction. The target turkey was 26 cents a shot, at 200 yards with an open sight. First prize was $10 and second was $5. The poorest shot of the day got a quart of whiskey. One might wonder which was the better incentive in a camp such as Jerome.

Another source of relaxation for men was a sportsmen's club. Some upstanding citizens, including a bar owner, merchant, and gambler, arranged to "plant" 300 small bass in Peck's Lake. The lake was at that time free of weeds. It was a home for ducks as well as birds, such as doves and quail. Jean Allison, one of the early members, continued the practice of planting various species of fish at popular fishing holes in the Verde Valley and the Oak Creek area. Hunting and fishing were to remain excellent diversions.

Jerome people traveled by horse and wagon to Sycamore Canyon, Oak Creek and the rim country, often seeking cool shade in the hot summers. Some purchased cabins among the tall trees, using them as get-a-ways from the stressful conditions of an active mining life. Johnny Summers, operator of a hauling company located on Hull Ave., purchased property east of Packard's ranch near the entrance to Sycamore Canyon. It was called "Dragoon Canyon Park, Jerome's New Pleasure Resort." There was a spring and stream for fishing. Summers planned to make good roads and open it to the public. It was located 12- 16 miles from Jerome.

The sportsmen also organized the Jerome Boat and Gun club,

*Deception Gulch watermelon party c. 1905*

*Delivering groceries to the Gulch c. 1905*

building club and boat houses at Peck's Lake. Baseball games were also held on the flat land around Peck's Lake. Many families would gather for a day's outing.

Glenellen Minty recalls the wonderful picnics at Pecks Lake. Her father, Courtney, would drive the carriage with a team of bay mules. He would pick up family members Laura and Walter Miller, the Minty grandparents, and all the food, and off they would go down the hill. Glenellen would often sit between her father's knees, hold the reins and drive the mules. The ladies would spread out the robes under a shade tree while the men went fishing and the children played. Late in the afternoon they would load up the carriage and start the long trip uphill.

Another sport not thought highly of was badger fighting. An editorial item in the JEROME NEWS of March 5, 1910 is a tongue in cheek story:

*"A badger fight was pulled off last night at the same old stand. It was the same old badger, too, and he had been well fed for the occasion. Aside from a dent in his ribs, the result of a hard fall in the last fight, he was in excellent shape. Ed Buehler, an experienced handler of badgers in his old home in the Hoosier state, pulled the chain. Charley Dunham [well-known local wall painter] will give the animal a fresh coat of paint and set it under his bed until another wise gazabo floats in."*

The sport had flourished for years, and while this newspaper article brought frowns by fighters, the game continued in the valley for a number of years.

Athletic clubs were started, advocating boxing, and wrestling matches which were held in the Opera House. Jerome also had a football team which successfully challenged various towns. Other men's groups formed were the Knights of Pythias, the GAR, the Mingus Tribe of the Red Men, the Copper Lodge of the AOUW, Masons, Elks, Knights of Columbus, and the American Legion.

People in Jerome came from many nations. Jerome became a small melting pot of different nationalities and ethnic groups. Many formed lodges, or societies, to bond their lives to the old country and their heritage.

In April of 1899 members of the Hispanic community formed Jerome Lodge #13 of the Mutual Society of the Alianza Hispanio Americana Institute, whose headquarters were in Tucson. The local lodge was to remain an important factor in the lives of the Hispanic community into the 1950's. In 1915 the Liga Protectora Latina was formed as a funeral society. Another created later to help families of dead workers, was the Sociedad Regular Colectiva Funeraria y de Ohorro.

In 1901 the Croatian Fraternal Union, Jerome Lodge 138 was created by the natives of Croatia who had taken advantage of the opportunity to go to America to build new lives. The Croatians were known as strong, hard workers, willing to take on the most dangerous jobs above or below ground. In 1894 leading Croatians

*Alianza Hispanio Americana float c. 1920*

*Rosemary DeCamp, movie and television actress*

in Pennsylvania organized the society to help families in the event of an accident or death. The Jerome lodge was made up mainly of Croatians, with some Serbians and other Slavs. It went up as high as 130 members depending on the fluctuation of copper production.

In the 1930's the Italian community organized the Cristoforo Columbo Lodge to assist Italian residents in times of need.

The town as a whole celebrated three major holidays: the Cinco de Mayo, Fourth of July and September 16th. The townspeople decorated their homes and buildings with bunting and flags preparing for the occasion. On the Fourth of July local bands played in the bandstand in the center of town. Often Main Street was closed and games, races, greased pig contests, and the drilling contests were held. There were also horse races, sack races, egg races and a race up Cleopatra Hill to water tanks. In the afternoon was the Fire Department's hose cart races and at night there were fireworks.

Miners, like cowboys, often, on holidays, played work- related games, such as mucking races and drilling contests. The JEROME NEWS reported an accident during the September 16th celebration in 1911:

*"James Kennedy, one of the drillers, received a blow on the head from a hammer, which accidently broke, and caused his death a few days later. Kennedy, who was drilling with Charley Shull (both expert drillers and held the championship of this district), was holding the drill when the hammer broke, on a downward stroke, and struck him a terriffic blow on the head. . .The force of the blow did not render Kennedy unconscious, in fact, did not affect him the least particle as he kept on drilling with his associate until the time limit and the team won the first prize of $140 cash. After dividing the prize Kennedy left for home and on his arrival there complained of severe pains in the head. He soon became unconscious. . .An operation (was) performed and the skull was found to be fractured. Mr. Kennedy lingered in an unconscious state until Monday, when life became extinct."*

Accidents at play were oftentimes smaller examples of those at work. The Hispanic community planned for weeks for Cinco de Mayo and the September Independence Day celebration. They would hold dance benefits in the Opera House to raise the money for the parades and lavish floats. The prettiest Mexican girl was elected by a contest to reign over the festivities. She rode at the head of the parade, followed by beautiful floats, bands, Boy Scouts, and later World War I vets.

The parade course started at the curve next to the Mexican town, the Barrio Chicano. It proceeded down to the United Verde Extension Mine where it turned and took the road that went to the West end of the Hogback. There it started back up the hill onto Main St. The queen dismounted from the float and was escorted to a decorated platform which had been construced right in front of the Opera House. In later years it was built, by the mining company, on Main Street in front of present-day Paul & Jerry's Saloon. Patriotic speeches began, given in Spanish. Music, food and games continued throughout the day, which climaxed with a ball at the Opera House until dawn.

Theaters and movies were also favorite sources of entertainment. Images, sounds and stories were placed on the screens of no less than six movie houses in Jerome's past. The earliest movies were shown in 1896. The machines were the old kind with flickering images of travelers in wagons struck on the railroad tracks, pushed to safety by heroes, and the big 'Chase' going on for mile after hilarious mile.

Early stage and movie shows were held at the Zaragosa Theater on upper Main Street, run by Santiago Tisnado. Spanish movies were shown as well as live performances of Zarzuelas, Spanish operettas. Zarzuelas were brought to Jerome by Manuel Areu. His son-in-law, Palemon Bablot, and company performed "vaudevilles" between films at the Lyric as well as the Zaragosa. The operetta consisted of spoken dialogue alternating with set musical pieces celebrating Spanish life, which was characterized by the romantic idealization of urban and rural life of middle and lower class Spaniards.

The Coliseum and the Electric Company theaters were also located on Main Street., playing silent films. The Coliseum was owned jointly by Bill Haskins and Phil Pecharich. When their partnership ended, Haskins opened a theater in the new town of Clarkdale. Pecharich expanded his entertainment empire of bars and restaurants to include the new Liberty Theater.

Construction was started on the Liberty Theater in April, 1918. Work did not go smoothly due to the Spanish influenza epidemic that year. It finally opened during the 1918-19 winter. The name, "Liberty", had been selected from those submitted by school children. It was patriotic considering the War To End All Wars was on. The Liberty originally had a concave nickelodeon-style front, with a ticket booth in the center. The entrance was on the east side, leading to the main floor or the balcony. The theater, which still stands on Jerome Ave., was built at a cost of approximately $80,000. This was reportedly recouped in the first year of operation. Advertisements from 1919 tell of two shows daily, 7:30 and 9:00. Admission was generally 30, 20 or 10 cents for main floor, balcony seats, or children, respectively. The instrument played at the Liberty Theater to accompany the silent movies had 90 stops, like bells, thunder, pistol shots, etc. The cue cards would come with the film. The piano player would get it the night before to coordinate the song to the scene. For a day's work the player often made $4.

In November of 1918 John D. Johnson bought the Joseph Thorbeck building, on Main Street. Johnson and his cousin had been running the Modern Cafe. They planned on extending the existing building to Hull Ave, making it about 137 feet deep. They also added another story. When they purchased the building, the Jerome Mercantile Co. was on the first floor and the Miners' Union was below the Main Street level. The cousins built an elaborate silent movie theater, opening in March of 1920. They noted that "talkies" were coming, and prepared to add sound equipment. The mortgage was held by the Bank of Jerome. It failed in the middle 1920's, leaving the Johnsons with many financial problems.

The novelty of sound films proved to be a death blow to the Liberty. Pecharich took advantage of the Bank of Jerome's failure and leased the Lyric Theater. He eventually bought it and changed the name to "Ritz". The Ritz opened with newly upholstered seats, on November 14, 1929. The Liberty was closed as a theater by early 1930. The first floor interior and facade were changed. Pecharich rented the street level as a cafe. The main theater room and balcony have remained pretty much the same ever since.

From time to time movie companies would take advantage of the wide open spaces and sensational scenery in the Verde Valley area. Movie star Rosemary DeCamp, who grew up in Jerome and whose father was General Manager, recalls scenes from her childhood in her book WIND 'EM UP:

*"One year Harry Carey came to Jerome and made a picture called "East is East" about a tenderfoot easterner trying to make it, in old Arizona. Everyone in the town felt involved becaused they used some of the mining camp people in the crowd scenes.*

*"One night my folks bundled me up and took me down to the old mine shaft where the company was shooting. I was pretty young and sleepy, but I'll never forget the sizzling white lights shining down on the leading lady. She was sitting on a pile of rocks by the mouth of a tunnel. At first I thought she must be an Indian because of all the paint on her face, white and black, and her eyes were rimmed all around with blue. Her mouth was dark red. Her hair was pretty though, kind of fuzzy-blonde and long. The best part was the accordion music. They had a fellow there playing gypsy songs. It sounded so lovely in the warm night. My mother explained that the actress had to cry and the music was supposed to bring tears. Well, sure enough, as soon as the camera started grinding, that girl's eyes ran rivulets. Some of the paint ran, too. Then they would stop and mop her face, paint it some more, and do it all again. I finally fell asleep, but years later when I had to weep in front of the camera, I wished for that gypsy music.*

*"The best part of the Harry Carey episode was the 'take-off', my dad and some of the mine executives put together. It was called 'Yeast is Yeast' and was all about a moonshiner and his daughter being chased by the 'revenooers.' I don't know how it got filmed and processed, but the result was weird. It was all black and white, no grays, and very jerky. My mother said it made her seasick to look at it. . .kind of like some of the 'hand held' jobs we see today."*

The Jerome newspaper, VERDE COPPER NEWS, wrote extensively about the "home grown, home written, home acted, and home filmed picture." E.E. Kunselman, a cameraman from Phoenix, was employed to film, develop, edit, and make subtitles for the movie. Many well known people of Jerome were drafted as actors. The filming started about 10 a.m. at the Jerome Transfer company barn by the Hotel Jerome. Miss Ann Housten, Scotty Mitchell, Matt Shea and other members of the troupe were made up at photographer Gottlieb's studio under the direction of Miss "Doc" Davis formerly of Universal. The VERDE COPPER NEWS tells the gist of the script:

*"Scotty sold his elaborate cowpuncher outfit to Matt for $10, retaining only his trusty revolver, presumably because he wanted to find which end the bullet came out of. He kissed the burro, Isador, a fond good-by, and went away to spend the tenner."*

"Yeast Is Yeast" was shown in Clarkdale but not heard of since.

During World War I, the mining town became a prosperous two-mine town where people's spirits were light and flirtatious. The United Verde Extension mining company had struck ore just in time for the war needs. There were more single professional people in town desirous of social activities. Teachers, usually young ladies fresh out of Arizona and other states' Normal Schools, were considered very important in the social activities in Jerome. There were also a number of young geologists and mining engineers from Yale, Carnegie Tech, Michigan, and Golden, Colorado mining schools, brought specifically to work on the open pit project at the United Verde.

Ellen Hopkins, school music teacher in 1916 and 1917, found living accommodations limited. She and a roommate were allowed to temporarily live in the Guild Hall of the Episcopal Church, which was located on the mine road. The young engineers and geologists would take the opportunity after work to stop in for tea with the eligible young women.

The new teachers were escorted by "old-timers" to the Opera House to attend the first dance of the school year. There they would meet, formally, the eligible young men working at the mine. Dance programs were filled within minutes, and arrangements were made for further get-togethers such as hikes, picnics and dances.

In August of 1917, while on a hike to Mescal canyon, two young Jerome ladies decided to refresh themselves by taking a dip in the stream. A monsoon-caused flood occurred, taking their belongings along with the water downhill. An ad in the classified section of the August 27th JEROME SUN read:

*"REWARD: for the shoes and stockings and other wearing apparel belonging to two young ladies who were bathing in Mescal yesterday just prior to the flood. The owners are willing to pay good and substantial reward for the return of same as they are keepsakes."*

*The next days SUN ran the following ad:*

*"WANTED: to know what reward will be given the person who finds*

*the clothes which were lost in the flood in Mescal Canyon Sunday. Certain gentleman would be glad to attempt search if the reward is sufficient. Will the lady please furnish information, who lost the garments?"*

And the day after:

*"REWARD: The young ladies who lost their wearing apparel last Sunday in Mescal flood beg to say that pleasure is its own reward and the person who finds their clothing may have the pleasure of returning same to them."*

B. Brooks, writer of "Babbling Brooks in the Desert" column in the same issue of the SUN, ends the drama with this quip at two adventurous mining men in town:

*"They say around town that Tom Finnerty and Louis Ferber are in on that reward for the clothes that were washed away. Some doubt if the clothes were washed away at all. Just keep your eye on Tom Finnerty and Louis Ferber."*

Owing to the town's prosperity, parties and dances became more lavish and frequent. There were 3 or 4 young men, calling themselves the Jolly Bachelors, who alone ran dances almost every other weekend. They saw a need and organized the events, hiring local bands to provide the music.

Another active group in town was the Business and Professional Women's Club. Helen Beck Droubay, who came as a new teacher, was a member and remembers some of the fun:

*"Many of the married women in camp were ex-teachers or ex-nurses so there was a feeling of companionship and unity. . .The new teachers and nurses soon joined. The club members met once a month for dinner, business and bridge. The mining company paid a very good cook to prepare the dinner and it was held in the clubhouse the company provided.*

*"We had a Bride's Dinner every spring, not long after school was out. There were nearly always quite a few weddings at the end of the school year. A special dinner was prepared, and a special table was arranged for the engaged members. They were given a program of skits, dances and songs. We worked for a month or so making parodies on the popular songs of the day.*

*"One year, the Business and Professional Women's Club decided to give a masquerade ball with a pirate motif. The company sent their carpenters to Miller's Hall and they made port holes out of all the windows and painted old tires as life preservers and hung them in the hall. They even constructed a gang plank from the street to the entrance of the hall. We ladies collected barrels and old bottles as decorations. With everybody in costume, it seemed to release all inhibitions, and the affair turned into a bigger brawl than the "Fireman's Brawl." One lady said to the school superintendent, 'Did you see how drunk Miss Burns was?' 'No, I didn't,' he answered. 'I guess I left my glasses home.'*

Members of the group rented a room provided in Sauer's Telephone Company building on Clark St. They would have card games and other social activities. Card tables and chairs were furnished, but the silver, dishes, linen and food had to be brought in. Many other dances were held in this facility.

The Business Women's club opened an employment exchange at the club room to bring together, without expense, women who had work to be done and women who were anxious to secure employment. Competent and worthy applicants would be sent to prospective employers as all would be investigated by Miss Buckley, the Red Cross nurse. The club also had a student loan fund.

New men's and women's organizations were formed, adding to the enjoyment of the increasing population in Jerome and the Verde Valley. The Jerome Lodge No. 1361 of the Elks was formed in 1919. A town census was required before they could be organized. One was taken by the Town government. It showed a population of 8409 persons, in town. The Elks' peak membership came in April of 1926 when there were 451 members. When the United Verde mine closed, the lodge moved to Clarkdale and is still active there. The Elks also had a scholarship fund for Jerome students.

The Alexander Moisa Chapter of the American Legion held dances and benefits in the Opera House. It dissolved shortly after the United Verde closed in March of 1953.

In November of 1922 the Rotary Club of Jerome, forerunner of the Verde District Rotary Club, was organized. It was admitted to membership in Rotary International on Jan. 3, 1923. Good deeds by this group include student loans, a junior baseball team, free employment agency for boys and girls, child welfare efforts, Community chest and civic welfare, highway safety, and a golf tournament and picnic. The women sponsored the local Camp Fire Girls, Fourth of July fireworks, Home Defense, March of Dimes, Heart Fund, Rotary Fund, Civil Defense. The group was renamed the Verde District Club in 1951 in Clarkdale.

The Kiwanis of Clarkdale-Verde district was formed in June of 1925 at the Legion hall in Clarkdale, and still exists.

With automobiles becoming more economically possible, Jerome turned more and more to the Valley and its rims for outings. The road to Stoneman's Lake outside of Flagstaff was being put in first class condition. Stoneman's lake was a favorite outing place for people of the Verde district because of its excellent fishing. Valley rodeos began in May. Valley roundups were held at Spring Creek, White Flats for the Upper Oak Creek round up, and the T-Bar roundup at Camp Verde. The Clarkdale Country club opened a golf course in 1917. Later another 9 hole course was created and a clubhouse built. A bull fight was held in Clarkdale by the river. It was not well received, and that was probably why it was the only one noted in the local newspapers.

In May of 1922, the Federal Forest Service appropriated money for building the necessary roads to open the top of Mingus Mountain within the next year. From the summit of the Prescott-

Jerome highway, there extends to the east a broad mesa, more than 1000 acres, that is almost perfectly flat. The proposed improvements included golf links, tennis courts, baseball grounds, cottage buildings, and a fine clubhouse. The highway between Prescott and Jerome had been realigned and graded in 1920, offering a better route between the two towns. A road to the top of the San Francisco peaks was started, later laying open the mountain top for winter sports. Another favorite picnic spot was Montezuma's Castle, which was, at that time, a magnificent Indian ruin, not yet a National Monument.

The Verde Hot Springs Hotel company announced that it was building a hotel to be ready by November 1, 1928. It was located about 35 miles from Jerome. The curative properties of the Spring water had been known for years, and would be available for the guests of the hotel in baths and for drinking.

A permit to hold wrestling matches within the city limits was granted by the Town Council. In 1936 a Town Boxing Commission was established. Boxing, wrestling and baseball were always favorites among Jerome men, especially those who liked to gamble on the outcome. A well-known fight promoter opened a barber shop in Fischer's Pool Hall on Main Street. The American Legion formed the Verde District Athletic Club, planning on promoting fights. The fighters had names such as Battling Curly, T-Bone Firbo of Jerome and Kid Chow of Prescott. While a favorite with the men, women of the town had trouble seeing the attraction. A VERDE COPPER NEWS issue of April, 1920, printed a letter from one female spectator. We offer excerpts from "Bestial Brutality of Beefy Bruisers Brings Blush to Bessie's Brazen Brow":

*"Dearest Anna: If you will promise honest to gawd not to tell ma or any of the home folks, specially Rev. mister Esop Hucklepenny, I am agoing to tell you a secret, and I rely on you as a lady not to tell anybody. Except maybe Geraldine and Helen and of course the boys. Now don't throw a fit I know you are a excitable nervous sort of girl not a bit like me always calm and cool like a horseradish. Well, I been to a prize fight! Last night there was a swell film in town, and I says to Frank, lets go and he says have you plum forgot there is a fight at the opera house and I am going. And what am I agoing to do all the evening I says and Frank uses a sware word and says all right I suppose you can come along but I should think you would rather stay home and read the Ladies Home Journal, he not realising about woman's rights and hunger strikes and everything. Well, we went and had seats right next to the ring and what do you think, Anna, there ain't any ring at all its a square platform with ropes tied around it all decorated with red while and blue real tasty like the handkerchief booth I and you had at the busy bee bazar. Only there wasn't any handkerchiefs at this affair, and when they began to get bloddy noese I reached mine up to one of them poor fellows, but he didn't have any pocket or handbag to put it in so he had to get along without it. But I am away ahead of where I am.*

*You can imagine how I felt, me teaching in Sunday school and past*

43

*exalted junior sister of our chapter and everything, and there I was just like one of these here demmy mondanes or vamps or adventuresses, and me a respectable married woman. I had on my new crape desheen and a large leghorn hat faced with pink which always brings out the natural bloom I am forced to use on my cheeks since the flu and being married to Frank... Well Frank says going home you have seen three good clean fights Bess and I give you my word Anna I never saw such a dirty bloody crowd in my life as these boys were when they finished each other. But you know how men are Anna only of course you don't but it isnt your fault that you are nearsighted and wear a No. 46 and I always did say you had a grand character. Fondest love from your true friend Bessie."*

Jerome in its best days had a champion basketball team and leading baseball club. In May of 1925 the Northern Arizona Baseball League was organized. The United Verde supported baseball teams in Clarkdale as well as Jerome for a number of years. The sister cities became quite competitive. Once a professional player, Hal Chase was hired as trainer. A big controversy started because Chase had been banned from major league baseball for his involvement in the 1919 Black Sox scandal. The Jerome team's winning that Fall pacified the people who had objected to the hiring of Chase.

Later only one Verde Valley team was formed. The Copperheads were headquartered in Clarkdale. Jerome maintained its home team, the "Miners", which was in the minor league. Other teams were incorporated into a Twilight league made up of the National and American leagues. In the National were: Miller's, Miners Meat Mkt., Steamshovel, Selna's grocery. The American league consisted of Scott and McMillan, Service Drug, Speakezy club, and the Victory Grocery nine. Games were played on the Clark Field located on dump land out Perkinsville Road (now site of the Gold King Mine Museum), and the 300 level diamond near the swimming pool and tennis courts.

The United Verde company provided three swimming pools for Jerome. In 1922 the first, located 3 miles outside of town on the road to Prescott at Walnut Springs, was opened. During summer months many people packed lunches and walked out the road or the more adventurous hiked up Hull's canyon past the Verde Central mine to the cool, popular swimming hole.

In 1928 a large pool was opened on the 300 level. The area became so crowded that the company felt compelled to make arrangements to control the use of the pool. The headlines emphasized the separation of the "Races". It was announced in the August 10, 1928, VERDE COPPER NEWS that:

*"...due to congested situation of new swimming pool at 300 level separate periods have been set aside for swimmers of the American and Mexican colonies. Beginning next Sunday night, the water will be changed and the Americans will be permitted to use the pool exclusively until Thursday noon, at which time another water change will be made and the Mexicans will have the use of the tank until Sunday night. This system will be followed throughout the summer. The United Verde Pool*

*at Walnut Springs will be conducted as usual with no special periods set aside for segregation of races."*

At the same time a pool in the Mexican neighborhood by Juarez and Conglomerate Streets was being built. It was advertised that a clubhouse was also being built. The opening made the newspaper:

*"The pool is identical in construction to the American pool on the 300 level, the change room containing every modern convenience is provided in close proximity. The length of pool is 30x70 feet, depth 2-1/2 to 9-1/2."*

Alfredo Mayagoitia read Mr. Tally's message:

*"Many of our oldest and most faithful employees, many of our best workmen, many of our valued friends, are members of the Mexican colony. We take pride in the fact that you are good citizens and are always ready to work and support any movement for the public good."*

The Mexican community continued to have organizations separate from the Anglos. The Gloria a Juarez No. 20, a Mexican Masonic lodge, was formally installed in 1928 at the Miller lodge rooms. It was named in commemoration of a Mexican hero. The Anglo Masonic Order joined with this new lodge in celebrations.

Mexican Boy Scouts troop was formed in February of 1928. In early 1926 a Boy Scouts camp at Peck's Lake, named Camp Taylor was created. Forty years later the Town of Clarkdale leased and turned it into a recreation & picnic spot. The Jerome Scout Troop No. 223, formed in 1917, attended state gatherings, often bringing home trophies from field days and round-ups.

The Hispanic people, adults and children provided much music for the people of Jerome from night serenading to organized bands and orchestras. Juan Ortiz and Alberto Castaneda promoted a youth band to continue their playing music during the summer. It was called the Reception Band because it practiced in Barragan's Reception Pool Hall on Jerome Ave. Mr. Tally agreed to sponsor the band.

Lily S. Hernandez reports in her paper LOS PIONEROS MEXICANOS:

*"A professional musician, Anastasio Mercado, music professor in Mesticacan, Mexico, came to Jerome and organized another band with his countrymen, all were musicians in Mexico. This was called the "Miner's Band"...The Miner's Band played in town on Wednesdays and the Reception Band played on Sundays...They set up across the street from Paul & Jerry's on (a special platform)."*

They also performed at street festivals and dances. Another popular group was the Kopper Kids.

Hispanic social clubs were: El Club Orquidia, all girls; Santa Cecilia, catholic coed club; and El Club Deportivo for men only and including a Sports Director, Luis Najera, who had been a pro-boxer.

KCRJ was a 100 watt, 130 KC radio station which went on the air in Jerome on June 12, 1930. K-Charles-Robinson- Jerome was originated in the Charles Robinson Jewelry Store on Main Street.

45

*Jack Lynch and William A. Clark, III by the airplane they died in, 1932*

*John's Place, a favorite watering hole, 1941*

It was on from 8 a.m. to 6 p.m., providing records, news and announcements. A Spanish hour was established, which featured live music by local entertainers. A tower was constructed on the Hog back by the cemetery. Later the station was moved to a nearby house. Its programs were heard for miles around, and operated into the 1940's, under the ownership of the Stuarts of Prescott.

The sport of aviation gathered enthusiasm in the late 1920's. William A. Clark III, heir to the United Verde, was an advocate of flying, and of a major airport in the Verde Valley. His dream was for the valley to have an international airport. Clark and his friend, noted flight instructor, Jack Lynch, were killed in May of 1932 in a Sunday crash near the foothills. An airport in Clemenceau had been established in 1928, and a group of anxious aviators was formed.

Lois Ward, Prescott area aviatrix, tells the story of Manuel Guiterrez of the Jerome Victory Market. Manuel bought an Eagle Rock aircraft and got Ersel Garrison to try to teach him to fly. Evidently Manuel did not have the proper depth perception to land.

*"One day while flying around the pattern, the instructor told him to use a patch of weeds as a reference point on the ground and that could guide him to a proper approach. It worked so well that Manuel was inspired to fix a permanent aid to his navigation. He took a pickle barrel from his store, painted it, and hauled it out in his delivery truck to an appropriate spot beyond the end of the runway. . .as a white marker for reference. . .Everything went smoothly, his landings became classic. . .One of (his good buddies) moved the pickle barrel. Manuel had to execute a go-around. His approach was all wrong. Again he got instructions and learned to fly the new pattern. About the time he got the new approach perfected, one of the boys moved the barrel again. In his despair Manuel was heard to say 'son-of-a-gun! I just get the landing down pat and that barrel, it moved again!' Eventually he landed the aircraft in an arroyo at the end of the runway and smashed it."*

Not all flights ended in disasters. Air shows and air carnivals were held at the small airport. Fund-raisers were held, offering short, scenic flights to be paid according to the passenger's weight. The pleasure of flying is still enjoyed in the Verde Valley.

Meanwhile, back on earth, the Jerome Public Library was taking a firm hold on the new quarters in the old hospital, remodeled as a library and clubhouse in 1928. By that time it contained between 6000 and 7000 well selected volumes. It had been moved from a small facility in the Hampton House to almost half of the ground floor in what has become known as the Clubhouse Hospital.

At the turn of the century there had been Clark's Revolving Library which provided citizens with some reading material. A number of town women petitioned the Town Council to look into getting a Carnegie Foundation library. The attempt to interest Carnegie in Jerome was unsuccessful.

The credit for starting a public library has been given to Mrs.

Val De Camp. She started the present library in a small store room in the Hampton House. The work was entirely volunteer at that time. Most of the books were donated by the townspeople, and were old. The VERDE COPPER NEWS special Clubhouse issue gives credit to Mr. Val De Camp for getting the facility for the workers and other residents in the busy town. In the April, 1930 issue of THE MINING CONGRESS JOURNAL, "Recreation in the Verde District" by Noel Pegues, conservatively describes the Clubhouse in Jerome:

*"The clubhouse has a large men's lounge containing pool and billiard tables, a soda fountain and card room, a ladies' lounge and card room, and a small ballroom which is used for dinners and dances."*

Miss Pegues' article gives a 1930 description of the recreation facilities provided for the workers and citizens of Jerome, Clarkdale, and the entire the Verde Valley, which had been provided by the United Verde Copper Company.:

*"At Peck's Lake, around which the Verde Valley Golf Club course is laid, a public playground has been established. Swings, teeters, merry-go-rounds, and other paraphernalia for childish enjoyment have been installed. Similar equipment is provided in the public park on the 300 foot level in Jerome. Four swimming pools have been built and are operated and maintained by the copper company. At both Jerome and Clarkdale pools are provided for the Mexican population as well as the American. There are club houses at both towns for the Mexican employes, and these too are operated without profit by the company. Oak Creek Canyon, scenery, fine trout fishing, cottage resorts throughout the 12 mile canyon...Stoneman and Mormon lakes popular, bass and perch fishing, virgin pine forest, summer resort...Mingus Mountain, maintained by Forest Service and picnic benches, tables, fireplaces, etc., are provided by the company. The nine-hole golf course within a mile of Clarkdale...all grass fairways, and being built around Peck's Lake, has the only natural water hazards of any course in Arizona...beautiful club house, with men's and women's locker rooms, a large lounge, dining room and kitchen, dance pavilion, erected as a part of the William A. Clark Memorial ...both motor and row boats are housed at Peck's Lake, excellent course for the speedy crafts. There are four tennis courts in Jerome, located near the park and the swimming pool."*

During the lean Depression years at the beginning of the 1930's, these recreation areas became very important. The mining companies tried to employ as many men for part-time as possible. Families would go to the pools, playgrounds and tennis courts, socializing with others in the same situation. It was commonplace for midday or evening meals to be pot-lucks, each family contributing what it could. This is another part of Jerome's life found years later, in the 1950's and 1970's when times were again lean.

The Dynky Lynx Miniature Golf course was located in the Town Park area between the Bank of Jerome and Miller's Store in the very early 1930's. The property was owned by the United Verde, but the golf course was managed by D.L. Bouse. Its popularity was intense but short lived in Jerome. Such prefabricated courses were a phenomenon of the Depression. They were all over the country. The miniature golf craze came back in the 1950's, but by that time the Dynky Lynx had disappeared, replaced by grass, trees and shrubbery.

This Town Park area has always been a spot of relaxation and recreation for residents and visitors. In early days, wood and barrel benches were set up around the gazebo, where people could listen to the music or watch the parade or games on Main Street. The Workers Progress Administration workers of the late 1930's built a strong stone wall to hold up Clark Street, laid out a grassy park, and constructed the large stone steps we see today. These steps make excellent seats for the Main Street show.

Another valley resort was called Geary Heights. Patrick Geary had homesteaded land between Clarkdale and Cottonwood. His daughter Helen, who was an entertainer in Jerome, around Arizona and other states, returned in the middle 1930's and created a dime-a-dance club. There was a bar, restaurant, and 50 feet by 60 feet dance floor in the main building. There were also cottages one could rent for private entertaining. The waitresses wore skirts to the knees and were reportedly school teachers. Music was provided by a juke box and local bands, but out of town bands often played. There were other dance halls and clubs in Cottonwood, Clemenceau and Clarkdale, but Geary Heights was perhaps one of the most extensive for its time.

School activities were of interest to parents and other citizens. School programs often provided the only evening's entertainment. Sports were of interest, and occasionally bet upon. Plays and musicals were held in the High School auditorium. One successful production held in the Jerome High School in 1935, was a program complete with drill team exhibition featuring a magnificent display of flags. After the presentation, there was a dance at the Opera House. Jesus Franco was the director, and Socorro Sahagun, the baton-leader.

Children usually find their own diversions from school and home life. At the turn of the century and the next decade or so, some children up on the hill were required to take dancing, art, piano, and sometimes voice lessons. Traveling carnivals and circuses, along with local fairs and water carnivals at the pools, were special attractions. An amusement area off Hull Avenue was run for a short time in the early 1920's. Some activities not previously mentioned are: the Aztec Roller Skating rink at Clemenceau, another later in Jerome at the old Gulch school, bowling alleys, special interest clubs such as the Jerome Junior Philatelic Club, and the indoor target range of the Verde Valley Rifle & Pistol Club, located under the Lyric/Ritz Theater, with the entrance on Hull Ave.

*Looking south on Main Street, c. 1930*

*Dynky Lynx Miniature Golf Course, c. 1931*

Mining activity was quiet at the United Verde for most of the 1930's. The United Verde Extension was on its way out of business because of a lack of profitable ore. Stores were closing uptown due, in part, to a lack of business, and, in part, to the large amount of ground movement occurring. A combination of underground mining activity, large dynamite and black powder blasts, and water and other liquids added to the ground, contributed to ground movement. Many homes were lost due to the unsettling land. The effects were the worst in the commercial district. Dozens of business structures were damaged and eventually demolished in the area East of Main Street. The Lyric/Ritz Theater, located on that side towards Town Hall, had moved substantially by 1935. It was reinforced in December, but continued to slide dramatically. One could watch a movie and see the sky through the cracks in the walls at the same time. The Town government took steps to close it as a public place. Two professional opinions as to the building's stability were given to the Town Council.

A letter from Lester A. Byron, Architect, Phoenix, dated March 2, 1936 made this analysis:

*"I have examined the property known as the Ritz Theater, and operated and owned by Mr. Phil Pecharich, for the purpose of recommending to your honorable body such disposition as should be made of this building in the interests of public safety . . . (The) average slippage of bearing soil in this area is at the approximate rate of 1/2 inch down and 1/2 inch to East per month . . . (There has been) settlement in (the) pavement which was leveled late in 1935. Cracks in (the) East wall materially increased since last rain; (The) floor of (the) basement shows difference in elevation of 1'-8". . .In consideration of the above facts, the deplorable present condition of this structure, the rapid failure which has recently taken place, and finally in the interest of safeguarding public life, I recommend that this building be closed against occupancy of any nature and that it be torn down."*

T. B. Stewart, Jr. was another builder who had been involved with the construction of schools and buildings in Jerome and Clarkdale, including the Douglas Mansion. Regarding the Lyric-Ritz Theater building stability he writes:

*"In conclusion, I appreciate that Jerome offers some striking examples of the extent to which buildings may be racked and distorted without falling. In this case, too, while I believe the odds are all against it, this structure may stand for some little time yet. On the other hand, all indications and presumptions are to the contrary, and I must recommend against its further use for the present purpose."*

Phil Pecharich agreed to tear the structure down. By June 15th of the same year he had opened the 700 seat new Ritz Theater on the corner of Jerome and Hull Avenues. It was built from plans by Del Webb. This last active theater in Jerome was closed about 1950 and demolished as an unnecessary building within a few years.

The United Verde Extension mine closed in 1938. Workers moved to other mining towns or to California, seeking new occupations. Jerome's population fell drastically. As the rumors that the United Verde mine (now owned by Phelps Dodge) was going to close soon circulated, other people took the opportunity to leave. Some remained, content to remain in the small town which had provided them with so much throughout the years. Card games, socials, dances and clubs continued with less members. The Clubhouse was still open, as were the upper floors of the Miller building. Before and during World War II, there were still many recreational facilities found in and near Jerome.

In 1945 Phelps Dodge closed the Clubhouse. Mrs. Annie G. Minhinnick, the librarian, left for the coast. Mrs. Charlotte Gardner was asked to take over the library which was being moved to a room on Main Street under Miller's store. The salary was meager, $75 each month with another $300 allocated for new books, magazines and papers. To one like Mrs. Gardner who loved books and reading, there was no question of what she would do.

The company officials approached her again in 1949, this time discussing the closing of the library. The company could no longer pay a librarian. Mrs. Gardner volunteered to take care of it for nothing but there was a rule against volunteers. She suggested the Star Club of the Diamond Chapter No. 7 of the Eastern Star take over responsibility for the library. They did and she stayed on until she left Jerome in 1952.

The books were put into storage until 1958. The Jerome Historical Society turned over the old Music Store building on Main Street to the Town of Jerome with the provision that it will be used as a public library. Repairs were made and the books were moved again. Through the efforts of the Community Service Organization, the Friends of the Library, county and local government funding, and the free rent and utilities provided by the Historical Society, the Jerome Public Library still offers the joys of reading, now in the basement of the old Fashion Saloon.

In March of 1953, Phelps Dodge ceased mining production at the United Verde mine. Social activity almost stopped. Since the Town of Jerome was still incorporated, there were still civic duties and responsibilities to be handled. The people who wished to stay and help formed the Jerome Historical Society in the attempt to preserve and perpetuate Jerome and her colorful mining history. The Society and the Town became the Chamber of Commerce and initiated an intense publicity campaign to tell about historical old Jerome. With the mining wages gone, the Tourist Dollar was needed as another source of income to keep the town alive. Social activity centered on this goal and the creation of a mine museum in the old Fashion Saloon. A number of mining artifacts were brought into town and placed at various locations for the interested visitors. Town members wrote publicity, distributed it and made countless black and white routed signs advertising America's Largest Ghost City.

Pot-lucks and fund raising dances were held. The dances did not make much, but the people were united in the effort to save Jerome. The annual reunion, originally scheduled for Halloween Night was started in 1953. This homecoming is still attended by hundreds of ex-Jeromites who come back in October.

Newcomers "discovered" Jerome. They took advantage of the cheap houses for sale, and fixed them up. The town slowly stabilized. The Community Service Organization was formed by concerned citizens in 1966. Their objective was to help the town government with community projects which could not be supported by tax monies. One of the important fundraisers created was the Annual Home Tour started in 1966. This event is still being carried on in May by the CSO and the Chamber of Commerce. Money from sales of the Jerome Copper Camp Cookbook, sponsored by this group, go to help the water and sewer systems.

In the late 1960's more and more people, wandering and looking for a quiet place to live, arrived in Jerome. At first the young people were not accepted because of their hair length, their clothes and their style of living. They, the "hippies" as they were called, found their own friends to socialize with. The Town fathers and mothers, and these young people stayed separate for many years. Private social gatherings were conducted in homes. Occasionally pot-luck dinners were held. Uptown the two bars, now called the Spirit Room and Paul & Jerry's, never lost a beat. As in the early days of Jerome, it was still a city of booze drinkers. Juke boxes provided music for the customers and the teenagers now danced in Rock and Roll. While visitors to the town swore there were only a handful of inhabitants, the population actually was counted at a little over 200 at its lowest.

By 1970 the population was approaching 300. The town was still quiet, with at least three separate groups of people in residence. The old-timers from Jerome's historic past were one group; a number of artists and writers, new to Jerome and generally in their 40's and 50's, were another; and the third, the long hairs who had lived mainly in the Gulch but were gradually moving into the apartment houses uptown. Each had their own sources of entertainment. The Valley provided many clubs, theaters and activities from bars to bowling. And, of course, there was television!

Concern for the deterioration of the historic buildings and civic affairs brought the three groups together in the 1970's. They learned to trust each other, united in the desire to keep Jerome on its feet. Pot-lucks became larger, drawing in representatives of the various groups. Music was live at the bars. The Verde Valley Art Association, a cultural center in Jerome since 1953, drew more of the different segments together with opening nights and new art shows. Many of the newcomers were art-oriented. New shops were opened and the Jerome Chamber of Commerce was reorganized. It has sponsored many arts and crafts fairs, antique shows and an annual

*Hull Ave. entrance to Verde Valley Rifle & Pistol Club in rear of Lyric / Ritz Theater during demolition, 1936*

Music Festival held at the mine's 300 level, in the effort to draw more appreciation and revenue for Jerome.

The Jerome Volunteer Fire Department still has an annual dance. Nowadays it is a masquerade dance on Halloween. There is also a barbecue fund-raiser towards the end of summer. They don't pull hose carts around much any more. The men and women now have been trained in every aspect of firefighting which might occur in this town. Weekly drills keep them on their toes.

Jerome was designated an official United States Bicentennial City on her 100th birthday in 1976. The Jerome Bicentennial and Restoration Commission was started. It was intent on the stabilization of the Victorian houses on the hill and the United Verde apartments. The Historical Society joined in this effort by obtaining a ten year lease from Phelps Dodge on the buildings.

The Jerome Historical Society has remained an important organization, dedicated to the preservation and dissemination of Jerome's colorful history. Through its efforts, and those of numerous friends of Jerome, the entire town was recognized for its historical significance to the state and country, when it was designated a National Historic Landmark in late 1966 by the U.S. Department of the Interior. The Douglas Mansion had been opened as the Jerome State Historic Park in 1965. It had been donated to the State of Arizona by James and Lewis Douglas in honor of their grandfather, father and uncle.

There are not anywhere near the number of clubs and organizations existing for the entertainment of people in Jerome now as there was in its more active, boomtown days. There is but a ghost of its former population on the streets today. The buildings have been decreased by almost half. Yet, there is a feeling, an essence if you will, of the old, unique Billion Dollar Copper Camp still around. You will find it, like a spook at night, when you least expect it. How could there not be, with so much having been done, by so many, for so long!

## BIOGRAPHY

Nancy R. Smith was born, raised and educated on the East coast, but in 1970, followed an old dream to live in Arizona. She settled in historic Jerome in 1972 and became a part of the community bent on preservation of Jerome and its colorful history. In 1981, Ms. Smith entered public life when she became a member of Jerome's Design Review Board. She continued to volunteer her time by serving on Planning and Zoning and on the Town Council. For years she also was employed as Archivist for both the Jerome Historical Society and the Camp Verde Historical Society. She writes for several overseas publications as well as the JEROME CHRONICLE, the Historical Society's Quarterly, and has presented papers at four of the society's annual symposiums. Her papers have been published in the Tucson Westerner's SMOKE SIGNALS as well. In addition, Ms. Smith compiled a Design Review Guideline handbook which was published by the Town of Jerome and the State Historic Preservation Office.

Presently she is working in the legal field but continues to research history, the Verde Valley in particular, and works for the town of Clarkdale on its Heritage Conservancy Board. She has two daughters and one granddaughter and loves to spend her free time tinkering with cars.

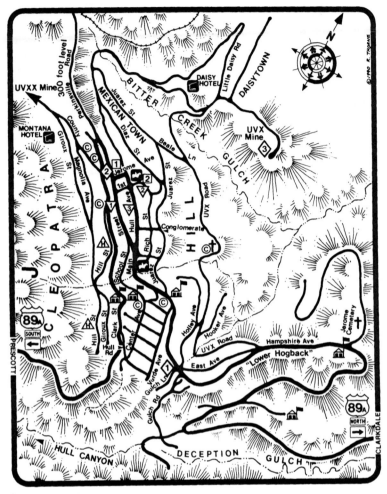

## OLD JEROME

◇ Points of Interest: 1) Fred Hawkins House, 2) T.F. Miller Co. Bldg., 3) Douglas Mansion.

▽ Jailhouses in order 1, 2, and 3

© Major Churches        + Cemeteries

🏥 Hospitals        ☐ Red Light Districts in Order 1 and 2

🏫 Schools        Livery Stables

Barbarick, Rick UNTITLED PAPER, p. 1.

Barbarick, Rick, INTERVIEW WITH LAURA WILLIAMS, May 8, 1972.

Brown, C.A., HISTORY OF JEROME, ARIZONA.

Brown, C.A., HISTORY OF JEROME, ARIZONA.

COCONINO SUN, Flagstaff, Arizona, July 21, 1918.

ECHOES OF THE PAST, VOL. I. Prescott, Arizona: The Yavapai Cowbelles, Inc.

ECHOES OF THE PAST, VOL. II. Prescott, Arizona: The Yavapai Cowbelles, Inc.

Erdoes, Richard. SALOONS OF THE OLD WEST. New York; Alfred A. Knopf, 1979.

Fireman, Bert M. ARIZONA: HISTORIC LAND. New York; Alfred A. Knopf, 1982.

Forrest, Earle R. ARIZONA'S DARK AND BLOODY GROUND. Caldwell, Idaho: the Caxton Printers, 1950.

Godard, Frank, INTERVIEW, JULY 28, 1990.

Hopkins, Dave, INTERVIEW, JULY 28, 1990.

Hudgens File, JEROME HISTORICAL SOCIETY

Hudgens, L. (wife of Johnny Hudgens) LETTER, HUDGENS FILE, JEROME HISTORICAL SOCIETY.

JEROME MINING NEWS, January 28, 1904.

JEROME MINING NEWS, January 28, 1904.

Jerome Newspapers: JEROME MINING NEWS, JEROME REPORTER, JEROME SUN, VERDE COPPER NEWS, VERDE DISTRICT SHOPPER.

Jerome Town Records, CITY TAX, AND COMMON COUNCIL MINUTES

McDonald, Lewis J., THE DEVELOPMENT OF JEROME - AN ARIZONA MINING TOWN, 1941, NAU paper.

Miller, Ronald Dean. SHADY LADIES OF THE WEST. Los Angeles: Westernlore Press, 1984.

MINING CONGRESS JOURNAL, April 1930, "Recreation in the Verde District,' by Noel Pegues.

Murbarger, Nell. GHOSTS OF THE ADOBE WALLS. Tucson, Arizona: Treasure Chest Publications, 1964.

PIONEER STORIES OF ARIZONA'S VERDE VALLEY. The Verde Valley Pioneers Assn., 1964.

Rudd, Eldon, INTERVIEW, JULY 23, 1990.

Shidler, Rosemary DeCamp, WIND 'EM UP, unpublished book.

Smith, Nancy R. PERSONAL COLLECTION

Smith, Nancy, WOMEN OF THE HALF-WORLD.

THOSE EARLY DAYS. Sedona Westerners, 1975.

Trimble, Marshall, IN OLD ARIZONA. Phoenix, Arizona: Golden West Publishers, 1985.

Trimble, Marshall, ARIZONA. Garden City, New York: Doubleday & Company, 1977.

Walrod, Truman. THE ROLE OF SHERIFF: PAST-PRESENT-FUTURE. Washington, D.C.: National Sheriff's Association.

Ward, Lois, M., EARLY VERDE VALLEY AVIATION . . ., 1985, Jerome Historical Society.

Willard, Don. AN OLD-TIMER'S SCRAPBOOK, 1984.

Williams, Sally Munds. HISTORY OF VALUABLE PIONEERS OF THE STATE OF ARIZONA.

Young, Herbert V. NEWSPAPER NOTES, JEROME HISTORICAL SOCIETY.

Young, Herb, Notes, JEROME HISTORICAL SOCIETY.

Young, Herb. GHOSTS OF CLEOPATRA HILL. Jerome, Arizona: Jerome Historical Society, 1964.

Jerome never died. Although its population dipped to a mere 50 souls during the late 1950s, by the 60s and 70s a growing emergence of newcomers began to arrive.

In recent years, approximately 400 artists, writers, musicians, historians and families now call Jerome their home. Most, attracted by Jerome's clean air and numerous possibilities, have shooed away the ghosts and taken over old abandoned homes and buildings, turning them into fanciful shops, alluring art galleries, comfy accommodations and delectable restaurants.

Working together with Jerome's old-timers, these inventive newcomers should be congratulated for aiding in the revitalization of one of Arizona's most fascinating queens of the copper industry. They have helped return her to her once glorious self. Although much about her is quite the same, Jerome has had a face lift... and adopted a new attitude. Because of this, Jerome is now a thriving art community and one of Arizona's most unforgettable tourist attractions. I believe Jerome's original founders would be pleased.

**Kate Ruland-Thorne**
*Publisher*

*Much about Jerome remains the same. It's just adopted a new attitude.*

*Restored homes and businesses still cling to Cleopatra Hill.*

*Main Street Jerome was once the theater district.*

*A popular Jerome restaurant pays tribute to Jerome's early-day shady ladies.*

*Photos by Kate and Keith Thorne.*

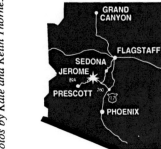

## About Jerome:
Altitude: 5248 feet
Founded: 1876
Population: 403
Ave. Annual Precipitation: 24.9 inches
Ave. Daily Minimum Temperature: 32.3
Ave. Daily Maximum Temperature: 89.2

Jerome Chamber of Commerce
(928) 634-2900

## ARTIST ROBERT SHIELDS
*Former Half of Famous Miming Team Shields and Yarnell*

"The reason I moved my gallery here is because I heard that Jerome was such a famous miMing community... that mimes were even underground and all over the place.
    WHAT? You mean I made a mistake? Those were *mines* - not *MIMES?*"

Shields and Yarnell.

*Charming shops and galleries abound in restored Main Street buildings.*

*The James Douglas mansion, built in 1916, is now the restored Jerome State Park and Museum.*

61

# HOW TO ORDER

*\*\*(Add 50¢ to each additional copy for postage and handling)*

| | No. of Copies | P & H | Total |
|---|---|---|---|
| **Experience Sedona Recreational Map** <br> *$4.95 + $1.25 Postage and Handling* | | | |
| **Experience Sedona Legends and Legacies** <br> *$8.95 + $1.75 Postage and Handling* | | | |
| **Experience Jerome** <br> *$6.95 + $2.00 Postage and Handling* | | | |
| **The Yavapai People of the Red Rocks** <br> *$6.95 + $1.25 Postage and Handling* | | | |
| **White Eyes, Long Knives and Renegade Indians** <br> *$4.95 + $1.25 Postage and Handling* | | | |
| | | | |
| **The Legacy of Sedona Schnebly** <br> *$4.95 + $1.25 Postage and Handling* | | | |
| **Wholesale Orders of 5 or More Copies Have a 40% Discount** | | | |
| *Tax 9.3% for Arizona residents only* | | | |
| *(checks or money orders only)* **Total** | | | |

Name _____

Address _____

Mail to: Thorne Enterprises Publications
209 RidgeRock Rd.
Sedona, AZ 86351

CPSIA information can be obtained at www.ICGtesting.com
Printed in the USA
BVOW071326190412

288037BV00001B/2/A